Also by Maureen N. McLane

Same Life

World Enough

My Poets

This Blue

FARRAR STRAUS GIROUX / NEW YORK

Maureen N. McLane

THIS

BLUE

Farrar, Straus and Giroux
18 West 18th Street, New York 10011

Printed in the United States of America
First edition, 2014

Library of Congress Cataloging-in-Publication Data
McLane, Maureen N.
    [Poems. Selections]
    This Blue / Maureen N. McLane. — First edition.
    pages cm
    ISBN 978-0-374-27593-8 (hardcover)
    I. Title.

PS3613.C5687A6 2014
811'.6—dc23

                                        2013033882

Designed by Quemadura
Photographs by Eric William Carroll

www.fsgbooks.com
www.twitter.com/fsgbooks
www.facebook.com/fsgbooks

1 3 5 7 9 10 8 6 4 2

Thinkers without final thoughts
In an always incipient cosmos . . .

WALLACE STEVENS
"July Mountain"

Species means guilt.

BRUCE ANDREWS

Contents

I

II

I

A SITUATION

Everything bending
elsewhere, summer
longer, winter mud &
the maples escaping
for norther zones . . .

Take it up Old Adam—
every day the world exists
to be named.

Here's a chair,
a table, grass.
A cricket hums
my Japanese name.

Skyscrapers
are stars. Rocks.
Those were swell,
seasons. So strange,
that heaven, that hell.

WHAT I'M LOOKING FOR

What I'm looking for
is an unmarked door
we'll walk through
and there: whatever
we'd wished for
beyond the door.

What I'm looking for
is a golden bowl
carefully repaired
a complete world sealed
along cracked lines.

What I'm looking for
may not be there.
What you're looking for
may not be me.
I'm listening for

the return of that sound
I heard in the woods
just now, that silvery sound
that seemed to call
not only to me.

AVIARY

Curmudgeon
pigeon,
iridescence
glinting unlike
granite,
what common
gullet did you peck
that crumb down now
you jerking thing
some call a flying
rat? Rats will inherit
the earth's garbage
dump and you
may also flash
on that trashheap
called the future
untransformed.
Yet to the dove
you're kin.
If my love
could sing

like a mourning
dove, could ring
the wrongs
away in the wind . . .
Kind bird,
do what's yours
to do with every
scrap forgot—
the nightingale's
not more precious
than your idiot
insistence to stick
around and peck and look.

OK FERN

OK fern
I'm your apprentice
I can now tell you

apart from your
darker sister ferns
whose intricate ridges

overlay your more
regular triangled fans.
Tell me what to do

with my life.

BEST LAID

it's clear
the wind
won't let up
and a swim's out—
what you planned
is scotched.
forget the calls,
errands at the mall—
yr resolve's
superfluous
as a clitoris.
how miraculous
the gratuitous—
spandrels,
cathedrals.
on a sea
of necessity
let's float
wholly
unnecessary
& call
that free

LATE HOUR

isn't it time
to say the garden
is wasted

on us? untended
roses the japanese
beetles gone

apeshit the labor
theory of value
will not redeem

the labor required
to reclaim
this. do I recommend

nothing?
I don't know
what to say

and go on
saying it

ALL GOOD

a "beautiful day"
nothing happened
and nothing was going to happen
the wind shook leaves
that did not fall
the moored boat did not sail
& the rain fell
on casual grass
everything was full
including the empty glass

*

a "beautiful rose"
no sign of a woman
but a boy's succulent anus
in a Persian lyric
call it ranunculus
or camellia
are they not more enfolded
than the folded rose
whose folds your nose
now probes

*

the mountain's

promiscuous

any cloud can take him

any sun have him

it's all good

today's assent

and tomorrow's

ANOTHER DAY IN
THIS HERE COSMOS

Stormthreat. Clouddarkened
mountain, computer
unplugged. Commuters
to nature on a plain

of grass the sheep
munch clear of clover.
A park's a way to keep
what's gone enclosed forever.

Rhyme is cheap.
So is pop.
Easy to be obese
in a land fat with rape.

Now the sun burns
unprotected skin.
Now the sheep dream
of lanolin.

To everything alive
we're kin.
Eat or be eaten—
what the vegan

spurns and the Jain.
I saved a fly
I baptized William Blake
and released to the sky.
Of course he'll die.

The new grasses
a brighter green
than the older spears
make this a scene

of summer starring
black butterflies. The Faerie
Queene alights from her magic car
a red convertible

and she a glam tranny.
The sheep don't care.
The sheep don't mind.
In three months the wind

will blow these trees bare
but for the tall pines
littering the forest floor
with browning needles

gone soft in the slow trample
of small creatures and long rain.
A park's a way to keep
what's gone enclosed forever.

SUMMER BEER WITH

ENDANGERED GLACIER

My one eye
does not match
the other

Corrective
lenses regulate
whatever

needs require.
Seeing?
I was being

being seen.
Let be
be finale.

Let our virtues
tally
up against

the obvious.
If we
don't believe

ourselves
custodial
why all

the hoobla-
hoo, hulla-
balloo?

Passivist
mon semblable
ma soeur

soi-même
blow through
this blue

II

WHAT'S THE MATTER

Why the low mood,
the picking at food?
Maybe it's the weather.

Maybe it's hormones.
Explanation's cheap
but sometimes hits the mark.

I am the target
of mysterious arrows
I myself let sling.

O that's your fantasy
of omnipotence.
You make everything
your thing.

All day I stayed in bed.
It seemed someone else
must have been alive

have done what I did.
Failed to do
what I failed to.

It's still in my head
those things I did
and said and cared for

doing but it's all gone
white like green hills
in certain light

as Dante says the hillsides
can go white
in the middle of a new life.

INCARNATION

Some are gay
in an old way.
It has its charms.

The kids are like
hey . . . wassup . . .
except they don't say
wassup. Hey.

The women with children
who are nonetheless
virgins. Mrs Dalloway.

The body a nest
of sockets
and unplugged cords.

The body without
organs has finally arrived
its wireless folds

almost tangible.
Years ago
I wanted to die

when you made me feel
we were fungible,
everything repeatable.

Later I floated
like a spirit
in a spirit photograph
above my life.

I shared a skin
with my skin.
I was in
my life not of.
I hovered above.

Then I descended
a millennial reincarnation
surprising myself
out of that ghost.

Carnations grow
in sandy soil.
You can touch
them. Hey.

TELL US WHAT HAPPENED

AFTER WE LEFT

Ferns here ferns there
I dream of my newest friends
who will soon subside
into near strangers
—peculiar the sudden
intimacies evanesced
without a kiss . . .

Who went home
with whom after the dance
party's what we want
to know. What century
did seduction
end in? Libertines
linger in the corridors

of the purely sexual.
I pulled you up

by my bootstraps
& liked it. I licked
you up & down

& up. I poached
eggs on your breasts
and combed yr curls.
There was nothing
I wouldn't do
with you & to.

Let's go down
to the river none
returns from. O yes
you swift diver
you plunge good.

THAT MAN

That man over there
looking sidelong
as you sidelong
smile I do not think

he's a god
or frankly that great
but it's true he's glowing
under your eyes &

obliterating
the sun that moments ago
was shining on this bench
where we sit across

from him now
flaring terrible
as I think of your
many rendezvous

I desire death &

I almost shove back
in my throat the call
to the Perseids calling them
down now to shower

him dead in their shower

EVEN THOSE

Even the places
the sun doesn't reach
in the deepest woods
are hot. Even the places

that never dry—the mosses
creeping everywhere
a damp carpet underfoot—
are dry. Even the quietest

places you've never been
are disquieted by your cry.
Even those places.

LUNCH WITH MOUNTAIN

The moss I ate
revised my esophagus
into a symbiotic system
any lichen could live in.
I ate too much
you sd last night
I could drown
from this beer
I can't finish.
Give me that stick
to shove down
my throat.
Give me your bow
your arrow
of burning burning
throated green.

THEY WERE NOT KIDDING IN

THE FOURTEENTH CENTURY

They were not kidding
when they said they were blinded
by a vision of love.

It was not just a manner
of speaking or feeling
though it's hard to say

how the dead
really felt harder
even than knowing the living.

You are so opaque
to me your brief moments
of apparent transparency

seem fraudulent windows
in a Brutalist structure
everyone admires.

The effort your life
requires exhausts me.
I am not kidding.

MORNING VANITAS

Weeding

the moss

a local

boy tends

the folly

the new gardener

created on the patio—

a loose

quilt of greens

the weeds' greens

are seen

to violate.

Every day

something

to exclude

to survive.

I cut

you out

of this

my life.

MORNING WITH
ADIRONDACK CHAIR

The woods are winds.
The rush of your mind
plays against a rustle
you could almost pitch.
Clouds a moment's
monument disperse
into an ever whiter sky.
Today you could be
anyone. A dragonfly
soars high above the grass
infested with annoying
flying beetles, bee-like
things made to sting.
You live your whole life
backward the green
chair always placed
there on the lawn
you long to flee.
Here it is—

another lawn
become a field
become a meadow
hedged with trees.
Why not sit forever
in a weathered chair named
for Indians you'll never
meet? Why the stand
of poplars marking the edge
of the town you arrive
at in dreams surprising
you back to the drugstore
the traintracks the road
out of town and also
back to its nuclear
bicycled streets?

Memory is boring
but as measure.
Everything is boring
unless it replaces time.
Music was making
me crazy
for a permanent

song nothing ever
unshaped I come
when you touch me
like that or like
that when you
move me into
an unforeseen
chair in your
exploding heart

GLACIAL ERRATIC

Boulders flung everywhere
signs of the glacier god
marking the path you can't take.

"I am in Brooklyn
but not of Brooklyn."
"Do you have an avidity
for the new?"

Some violence
is very slow
until it makes itself felt.
Makes you feel it.

"I need to write
good fast music.
All my good music
is slow."

How should a person be?
"I am happy

to be contemporary."
"I am glad I will die
before all this prevails."

In child pose
you breathe through the back.
Then there's the rest,
all those positions

you flow or stumble through
until that rock. That specific rock.

ROAD / HERE NOW

I think of you here
because I thought of you here
before. Otherwise
I never think of you

except on a summer drive
that echoes the drive
I took the day after
I heard you died

except when I see
the red skirt
I wore that day
the day you finally
kissed me

a red skirt
I now see
only in pictures
from a long-ago trip
to the Pyrenees

the skirt I wore
to your party

In the middle of the party
here's death
is what I thought
when we saw our friend
lying on the bare road
by her smashed bike

She's alive
in the Berkshires.
So many are alive!
More are dead.

Strange thing
to survive to discover
you will live
till one day it's over
no more to discover
no more rounding back
to this ongoing living
avoiding till you don't
that specific rock

III

TODAY'S COMEDY

Why Dante in summer?
Why not? The doctrine
of purgatory's no more strange
than nanotubes or Tang.

I used to know
its ins and outs.
What we've abandoned grows
higher than trashheaps

in Naples. My love
canal's clean and my heart
in my breast
is right dressed.

No guide led me here
but Virgil and everyone
I ever met, in woods
books dreams in suburbs

the city the farm.
Marcus Aurelius

took a page
from the town mouse

and his country cousin.
The lesson of fables
is mutable, their structure

not. Something
must change. A hero
must range in a land
he also unwittingly

charts. If many die
not everyone can.
Odysseus must reach
if not Ithaca

a farther shore
and the little zygotic blip
you once were
must enter the world

& its pure gore.

MEZZO

To choose

not to translate

heaven

paradiso

not so heavy

so let it be

& let there be

a Golfo Paradiso

sailed slowly through

the day you arrived

at the place the names

made their way to your ears

*

did all this fall

into the lap of the world

protozoa pulsing

upward from the slime

complicating themselves

into a sentience

you'd recognize

*

the quilted greens
an eye ascends
the terraced steep
attests the hands
and feet of men
who raised the sail
& crushed the grape

*

Apennines scraped
but for a few pines—
man or sheep or time
the denuder,
stripper of scrub,
flayer of rock—

*

that stone over there
whitestreaked outcrop clawed
by perpetual waves
it too thinks
a stone's stoniness

*

here it is ever
mild and the faces
show it gently
lined different
from the way
a less temperate clime
will incise you

*

below my neck
a faint network
the mirror reveals
in the morning

nel mezzo del cammin
I was caught
in a glass net
what did the glass weave

GENOA

The merchant republics are done
as is the nun
who forbade us aged five to say
we were done.
The oven door opened
in her mime
the door to the oven
where we were thoroughly roasted
and done.
If you are done
that means I can stick
a fork in you. You
she corrected
are finished.
Finished
with all that some days
it seems a dream
the long boredom
in the schoolroom
workbook assignments
rushed through straining

toward what weird

consummation?

Sister Lucretia—

she was another one

terrifying the children who braved

the zenana of nuns

pledged to Christ and torture

of the wayward souls who ventured

into the sanctum sanctorum

the private apartment of six nuns

for a weekly piano lesson.

Bach had twenty children

she declared. Her heart was given

to a Texan—Van Cliburn.

A wimpled nun

one of the last

thus to dress among the remaining Franciscan

sisters. Excess

daughters in immigrant families

ready to give some

aid and comfort to the Lord

or the local monsignor—

a special vocation—

were they rotting away

in their habits, were they
the transfigured ones?
I wanted once
to become one.
Those days are done
and I am almost done
almost historical as a usuried ship
heading west and more west
to find treasures
for kings. Look in thy heart
it is a treasury
it was said
Mary said.
She was another one.
Even now at the Brignole station
we see flocks of nuns
rope-belted, a crucifix flying in wind.
A veiled woman
might become another woman
under a different sun.
Even here the sisters
have become Indian, Ethiopian,
no extra Italian
daughters to pay the godly sum

of glorious renunciation.
The Turks are threatening Christendom
in old chronicles
and today's European bulletin.
Beware of falling under the thumb
of Islam.
It will never be finished
said the Caliph
to the Sultan.
It is almost done
this meal where I stick
a fork in tomatoed squid stew
called *burrida* its Arabic origins
brining my tongue.
I stick a fork in an animal
fork in a soul
and I eat and I eat
until kingdom come.

SAN FRUTTUOSO GLOBAL

The merchant republics are done.
The Cristo degli Abissi beseeches the sea
from seventeen meters below.
He will never again see the sun.

They sank him in 1954.
The Strada Nuova was old.
Genoa devoured the world, Braudel said.
Columbus killed Taínos for gold.

It's good not to be dead
—a thing one wouldn't have said
those days the islanders fled
to the hills escaping Spaniards

their helmeted heads
and fists clasped round handles
of pikes and swords for striking
off every savage hand

empty of glinting metal—
they knew they knew
where gold could be found
and they knew their lord

a forgiving lord
who watched indifferent
as they ran them to ground

DRINK WITH MOUNTAIN,

REMEMBERED, ANDALUCÍAN

The rosé from Spain
followed us west
as if hot on the scent
of tomato—

O brave New World
your fruits have gone incognito!
A rosé's a rosé's a rosé
with love apples.
You are moving west
beyond the Chinese coast
to the interior
of Inner Mongolia. A threatened
horse rides again

the steppes unburdening
themselves below revived hooves.
The time of the emperor
is nigh. No inquisition

will be able to check
the future. Your local
grapes are delicious

picked off the vine
or bottled, thus.
This is the interval
between eras of fathers,
dictators fallen, the marble
fists crushed and not crushing.

But the future, its empress,
who can say what beast
she'll ride to meet us?
Raise a glass, comrades—
all you who refuse
to forget the civil war.

INSCRIPTION

Not far
from the Chandrabar
and the Nervi Belvedere
I drink this beer
under an awning
on the Passeggiata
Anita Garibaldi
a kayak flotilla
choreographed quintet
heading east and easter
the French Alps outlined
in a faint blue to our west
My t-shirt's plain
white & cheap
an affront to the strollers
jewelried & jacketed
though here and there
a louche jogger
lowers the tone
almost to my level

& a young mother
& a posse of teens
newly gelato'd pass by
Serena Hearts Lucas
names on stone

TO ONE IN PARMA

The privilege
of even being
provincial,
to know the small
humiliating city,
the ever unfinished
cathedral,
that over there
is the real where:
we had none of it.
No one heard
of anything.
The glit and shine
and scut of it shimmered
on TV the satin crotch
of the metropolis
a 13" square
of already thinned
fantasy.
No wonder
the saints

were martyring themselves
repeatedly, furiously
in imagination.
This was something
to die for
a life outlined
in acid-bit etchings
obsolete as the names
of trees we were never given
to know in the neighborhood.

LEVANTO

salt lips & a buoyed band
binds the sea in loose chains
to swim in. the beach's
thinned out, the clouds puffing
in, the last ferry's
debarked a last load.
starting out now
seems impossible
but. the rock walls
break the breakers
in. nothing
cannot be disciplined
or freed. scant pines
stagger the apennines
semaphoring
what. quartz-
striped granite
tells a time
that outlives us.
I am older
than the sea
in me.

IV

TERRAN LIFE

—an excursion beginning with a line of William Wordsworth

When we had given our bodies to the wind
we found bones in the earth and not in the sky.
We found arrowheads in the earth and not in the sky though
   they'd flown through the air before grounding.
The era of common sense is over
& finished too the flourishing of horoscopes.
Hey traveler what chart to sign your way? what iPhone app?
All the birthdays have immolated themselves in a far pyre
and no one knows where
they were born.
Earth gods always come after sky gods.
If you could choose
a secret power would it be flight?—
a wish more often expressed
than the desire for invisibility.
"A mythology reflects its region"
and a poet sang the sea the lemon trees and pines
the Ligurian breeze salting his lines
and a lightly placed step on a Greek mountain is the goat song
   of tragedy.

Jehovah rarely shows his face for we would die of it
die as surely as those who looked to the sky in the bombing raid
the underground tunnels a sudden refuge
Out of ash I come   Out of the earth
Back to ash I go   He fashioned them
male and female I tell you
they wore the most beautiful evanescent clothes
in paradise so much subtler than the trawling nakedness of
     heaving giants
hurling other giants to heaven & some to hell
on the restored ceiling of the Sistine Chapel.

Thus far clones are of earth, alone.
When you say earth you mean land but more than land   You
     mean the oceans covering "the earth" as if earth were the
     substrate of everything and not also the crust.
I found the ground sound, unfaulted, uncracked, even where the
     continents have split and will again split the archaic seamstress
     unable to suture the plates of the earth forever.
"Terran life": what the biologists typically study but "weird life"
     is also a zone of research. "It is easy to conceive of chemical
     reactions that might support life involving noncarbon
     compounds"—
viz. *The Limits of Organic Life in Planetary Systems*, p. 6.

Earth now supports life but could not now initiate it.

Crawl, sway, sashay: you're still doing it on an earth

    you take for granted instead of going crazy

    yr head blown off by an apple no I meant an IED no

I meant an apple.

Newtonian physics' defunct but that doesn't mean an apple doesn't

    fall far from the tree composed of atoms whose dark matter you

    don't know how to measure, supermodel. Me neither.

Gravity thy name is woman

    always secretly pulling me toward you

    as if I had no resistance

    as if the clothes I wore were merely draped

    on a mannequin as if I were merely an earthbound species with

        new skin

    that fur an old animal's fur

    reclaimed by another.

Did you see the subtle shift from umber to somber to ochre on the

    walls of Les Caves de Lascaux?

What ibex steps as beautifully as you

what ancient bison shakes the steppes

what gazelle's ankles are so perfectly turned as yours?

There are no crackheads in prehistory but surely

they were addicted to something those hominids

strutting their way out of the savannah—

I demand the sun

shine on me

I demand the moon bare its face in the night

and lo! damn! see how these heavenly bodies do what they do

like clockwork before clocks

like skin before clothes

like the earth before the parting of the waters revealed

the earth was the earth is the earth . . .

And if she only likes vegetable things

that grow toward the light

and if she will not eat your roots and tubers

how then choose

between a rooting boar and an urban forager—

There is beauty in indistinct areas the microtonal

hover where the ear buzzes so—

There is a gasp a sharp breath in a sharp wind reminding

you the wind was someone's breath chilled.

Clouds are now fashionable as they were in John Constable's

    day Luke Howard having taxonomized the little buggers in

    1803: cumulus, cirrus, etc.

So let's go skying with Constable let's scan

the horizon as if we were sailors

able to read the sky   Let's blast off

and outsoar the noctilucent clouds
I espy with my little stratospheric eye.
Do you think I'm afraid of crashing to earth?
Love we've been falling ever since falling made way for a leap.

EMBROIDERED EARTH

embroidered earth
refusing an undesigned mind
uphold me now
it's hard to walk
secure on your pillowed ground

mossed ferned & grassed
this tapestried field
may it yield to an unsteady step
& take only the softest impress

the enfolded brain pressing
against a carapace
millennia ago unfolded
a species and its walk—
a steady upright walk

ICE PEOPLE, SUN PEOPLE

Something to it, the thought
of a people like its clime
or thereby impressed—
my lunchtime lassitude dissolved
the minute I moved from the sun
to this shadowed grass.

I could invent the wheel now
& soon the cotton gin
and steam engine &
let's not forget
it won't be long now
before nuclear fission.

Nothing's beyond
my airconditioned ken.
My offshore multinational's
humming more power
than the biggest powerstation in Hoboken.
My shadowed shade
my intemperate glade my big fat thrum.
Let's call it progress, this.
Let's call it whatever it is.

BELFAST

Your velvet hills came to me
last night in the pool
how they hugged the fraught city
the pubs filled and buzzing
the Europa unbombed now for years.
Your political murals are kitsch
and history's a ditch
for lying if we let
the gravediggers
name us. Let's bury
our pseudonyms
all undisclosed.
Was Scarlett O'Hara's father
a blustering Ulsterman
or was he a peasant
like granddad from Wicklow
tender and fond amidst the riot
and kind to his slaves
but for the obvious?
White people are weird
with their vitamin D

and sunravaged skin.
So far from an equator
it's hard to walk the line
in a cleaved world.
Orange, green, navy blue
the colors are weapons
as were some horses
in the 19th century.
Freed by machines
see how they race
on fragile ankles—
beauty a late flower
of disuse. Your storefronts
were boarded, your university
Victorian, the linen quarter
defunct. The solid brick
that shelters us unmortared
smashed a window.
Your sky hung low your beer
rode high your visiting Masons
sober and punctual.
A Days Inn here
is a Days Inn anywhere
but for the marchers gathering

their ribbons' gaud at odds
with their drawn gaunt faces
shut like a purse
around an old watch
that still keeps time

DEBATABLE LAND

The palest green immerings on the slopes
the snow'd made white near overspread
the snowdrops ungeared for fighting
yet strive they do to live in this suddenly
    coldened place.

The silence of the knowes rising above
St Mary's Loch is almost the silence
of nearby graves but the yow-trummle
pierces the mizzle we've decided
    to plow though.

Other people's disputes are not yours
till they are. Whose debatable land
did you walk on whose unmarked graves?
The village of free blacks buried below
    Central Park.

The Hanging Tree an English elm anchoring
a corner of Washington Square Park
knows nothing of the disintegrated dead
who long fed its soon-to-be
    commemorated roots.

Let's unpeel the world
and bite that big fruit the earth
it took us too long to remember
well-being just being holy land just land
the hanging tree a tree the son
of man a man.

THINGS OF AUGUST

Not fog not hail not sleet
but rain boring
as ever the same
rain less acidic
now the Midwest has failed
and new laws prevailed.

We shall abandon
our cars. We shall walk
unadorned under stars
whose names we shall learn
in four languages, minimum.
Our maximum velocity
will be no faster
than an average human can run.
Everything scaled
once again to the body.

The body? My amplified
brain's going haywire
not to mention

my juiced-up tits
and pumped lips. An army
of amputees marches
on Dacron prosthetics
the military should do better by.
I was nostalgic
until I got over it.

My diabetic sister's living
and a million women past
predicted deaths in childbirth.
Good. I can't think
my way out of this
covert. I'll just stay
here with the soft frightened
rabbits while the hunters
storm the brambles looking
for whatever today's kill might be.
Those hunters who fed
or still feed me.

REPLAY / REPEAT

Amazing they still do it, kids—
climb trees they've eyed for years
in the park, their bicycles
braced against granite hewn
hauled & heaved into a miniature
New Hampshire Stonehenge . . .

Your white-pined mind
fringed with Frisbees saucering
the summer into a common
past—look, it's here! two red
discs! & the goldplated trophies
everyone gets for team effort.

Human beings always run
in groups. Sure there's a solitary
walker, can't bother
him, iPod breaking his brain
into convolutions
you'll never get the hang of.

Go skateboard yourself.
My maneuvers are old-
school, yes, but so's school
& summer & children
& these fuckedup resilient trees
which tell time like the Druids
by the same old same old sun.

BROADBAND

Before I open my mind
to the sludge
the open connection
will carry

let me tarry
with archaic diction
and ancient bodies
the sun & my own

shaped by a code
unfolding itself
through millennia.
For thousands of years

art had no fashion
was the beautiful
drawing we did.
In cave after cave

the ochred bison run
by charcoaled aurochs
and a delicate ibex
an opposable thumb

grasped. Don't think
they've gone
from your mind

I remind myself
rousing from sleep
the screen of my brain

WESTERN

I can see the big sky
people have a point
the clouds mounting high
above the lake give

the lie to the fat claims
of mountains. The eye
requires a horizon
Thoreau somewhere sd.

Somewhere over yesterday's
rainbow the clouds compact
of mysteries rise
and billow, ample sheets

in the blue. The line
is an orienting
thing. The horizon
the plumb line the halyard

we tightened for good
sailing. How we want
the world rigged tight
yet not rigged against

us. In Texas Montana
Dakota they know it
the cattle rounded
up for decades

into a genre near dead
as the passenger
pigeons that famously
darkened the sky

HOROSCOPE

Again the white blanket
icicles pierce.
The fierce teeth
of steel-framed snowshoes
bite the trail open.
Where the hardwoods stand
and rarely bend
the wind blows hard
an explosion of snow
like flour dusting
the baker in a shop
long since shuttered.
In this our post-shame century
we will reclaim
the old nouns
unembarrassed.
If it rains
we'll say oh
there's rain.
If she falls

out of love

with you you'll carry

your love on a gold plate

to the forest and bury it

in the Indian graveyard.

Pioneers do not

only despoil.

The sweet knees

of oxen have pressed

a path for me.

A lone chickadee

undaunted thing

sings in the snow.

Flakes appear

as if out of air

but surely they come

from somewhere

bearing what news

from the troposphere.

The sky's shifted

and Capricorns abandon

themselves to a Sagittarian

line. I like

this weird axis.
In 23,000 years
it will become again
the same sky
the Babylonians scanned.

MOSS LAKE

I eat this silence
like bread.

The white lake
replaces my head.

I am cold & calm
as the untracked snows.

SKYWATCH

a brace of stars
a shivered benediction
of moon
Latin splashes
the firmament
as if it were universal
as the Milky Way
scanned by Chinese poets
& Egyptian astrologers

how not to fall
in the permanent black
unrelieved
except tonight
by this light

QUIET CAR

the willow's lost its hair
the snow's receded almost everywhere
and you are riding in the quiet car

the branches mostly bare
but the thin icesheets that cracked and chimed the pond
                        have vanished into water
while you are riding in the quiet car

walking around the reservoir
            canvasbacks gliding on the water
the path two miles, perhaps a bit more
while you are riding in the quiet car

soon I will climb in the old blue car
and drive to Back Bay, not too far
from you my love now riding in the quiet car

SONG

Love's in Gloucester
setting a lobster pot
in her mind.

Love's in Gloucester
feeling the wind's effect
on inner and outer shoreline.

Love's in Gloucester
where the whalers once sailed
and the cod's collapsed

but the sea the sea
calls to whoever
has ears for what's leaving and left.

HER SUMMERMINDEDNESS

Her summermindedness
embraces all full green things
& banishes nothing.

The dragonfly helicoptering
over the pond the deerflies
harassing the swimmers
& the leech on the leg linger forever.

Everything a scale
of clear intervals
no roadkill can mar.

The baby spiny thing
rubbing itself against
or was it scratching
the bark of a thin tree
by the roadside.

The speechless waddle
caught in the headlights

of late cars by the lake
moonlit and perfect
for canoeing in her summer mind.

O porcupine
spine in the mind
even a blithe summer mind
swerves from your shine

LOCAL HABITATION

The wildflowers
of New Hampshire
have yet to earn their names.
Flagrant apparent
they litter the meadow
casual sprays in patches
on the edges the gravel
almost reaches.
Sure there are
daisies and clover
beyond that
things remain
unspecified.
It seems rude
to pry. Elsewhere
it's called good
old simple asking.
Here wonder's
best kept secret.
Don't leak
your want

I've learned

not a native

but not wild enough

to resist

what constricts

a field

of uncut flowers.

THE FACT OF A MEADOW

North of Boston
roads diverge.
Downed birches
clog the Nubanusit.
A meadow made
a lightning field
by flashing flies
reclaims its green
each morning.
What the clouds now pass
you will not pass.
Those flies
were beetles.
Pine needles grow
in fascicles sewn
like Dickinson's poems.
A stone wall
stumbled on
stubs the mind

into an old ache—

what did you make

what did you make

of all diminished things

MÄRCHEN

The timbering done
the afternoon rings out
an aftermath.
What euphemism
would you not choose
in this multi-use
forest? I've left
crumbs for returning
the way back
marked by tiretracks,
lopped branches.
I've left words
in woods the thrushes
sing in refusing
the extinction
of the day. Pines
guard the path.
The way we come
back will not
be this way.

ELSEWHERE

The beer was nice
but not what we wanted
nor the rain nor the century
nor the actual children
we had. Let's not talk
about the parents. The forsythia
yellowed the hedges. *So there*
sd the spring. *So what*
the jay shrieked. A concussion
of air stripped the inner ear
vessels clean but for the gist
we needed to hear by.
A siren sang this evening's aria
after a basketball'd
recitative. In other places
other people thought through
different birds. They eat
dog meat there. We refrain
from outright condemnation.
Everywhere we know
the sun is setting
in an absolute sky.

ENOUGH WITH THE SWAN SONG

The woods are words
the turkeys spell
with their feet
their pine-needled path
a wild way
we won't take.
The sheep that bleats
in the night escapes
a starry declivity
we must be rescued from.
The rocks rest
below mosses, the pines
outtop the hemlock.
Flat ferns fan the wind
that will not break
this heat. I am lonely
with the sculpted edges
of fat leaves on low shrubs.
Ingrate soloist the chorus
is just beginning
and that bodacious robin
doesn't care if you join.

ENVOI

yesterday
I sat on a swing
and swung
will I do this for ever
will I never
not be a child
the grave
my last crib

*

I noticed to-day under a tree
nobody was singing to me

but oh there was singing
and there was that one tree

Acknowledgments

Thanks to the editors and publishers of the following
journals and forums, where some of these poems first
appeared, sometimes in different form: The Academy
of American Poets "Poem-A-Day" series, *The American
Reader, The Cortland Review, Grey, The Kenyon Review,
Literary Imagination, The New Yorker, nonsite.org, The
Paris Review, Plume, Poetry, Port, Psychology Tomorrow
Magazine, Shearsman,* and *The Wallace Stevens Journal.*

My deepest gratitude as well to the Liguria Study
Center for the Arts and Humanities / The Bogliasco
Foundation, the MacDowell Colony, and Yaddo,
which granted residencies that supported the writing
of this book. Their air is everywhere here.

To Jeff Clark, again. To Christopher Richards.
And to Eric William Carroll, of the blue line.

To Jonathan Galassi, compadre.

*   *   *

For L: *mio disio però non cangia il verde.*